Confessions From The Bathroom

Written and Illustrated By:
Martin Riskin

G000123889

Ivory Tower Publishing Co., Inc.
125 Walnut St., Watertown, MA 02172
Telephone #: (617) 923-1111   Fax #: (617) 923-8839

CONFESSIONS
FROM THE
BATHROOM

I admit it.

I admit that I think about bathrooms. I think about going to the bathroom, and what's more, I think about what goes on in the bathroom. Isn't that shocking?

A lot goes on in a bathroom that nobody wants to talk about. Some people won't even admit they go to the bathroom, much less discuss it.

I say, since everybody visits a bathroom at least twice every day, a lot of things must be going on. Nobody is willing to talk about it. It's a cover-up that makes the Watergate stonewall look like a wading pool.

The bottom line here is, a lot of funny things happen in a bathroom, and I'm here to tell about it. The result is the most riotous, ribald and embarrassing collection of dumps you've ever read.

More than enough to fill a book actually.

Every once in a while, each of us experiences a Perfect Dump. It's rare, but a thing of beauty in all respects. You sit down expecting the worst, but what you get is a smooth sliding, fartless masterpiece that breaks the water with the splashless grace of an expert diver. But that's not the end of it. You use some toilet tissue only to find that it was totally unnecessary. It makes you feel that all's right with the world and you are in perfect harmony with it.

THE
PERFECT
DUMP

Talk about nasty dumps. Depending on the dumper's tolerance, The Beer Dump is the end result of too many beers. It could have been 2 or 22, it doesn't matter. What you get is a sinister, lengthy, noisy dump accompanied by a malevolent fog that could close a bathroom for days.

THE
BEER
DUMP

Long, curly and perfectly formed like 2 feet of E13 telephone co-axial cable. It loops lazily around the bowl, like a friendly serpent. You wonder admiringly, "Did I do that? Where did it come from?" You leave the bathroom pleased with yourself.

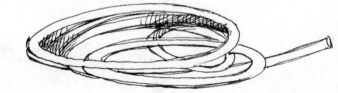

THE
CABLE
DUMP

This is the masterpiece of dumps. It's as perfectly formed as it can be. Delicate and slender with intricacies that would make da Vinci weep. And just think, you made it yourself. You may even want to break out the polaroid, but maybe that's going a bit too far.

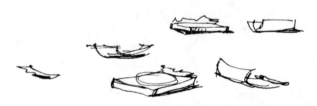

You're done... You reach for the toilet paper only to discover that empty cardboard cylinder. A mild panic begins coldly in your throat. You could use the curtains... No, someone would say, "Where are the curtains?" Then what would you say? The rug?... Too cumbersome. Then you must come to the same conclusion that every "empty roll dumper" must face... Pull up your slacks, tighten your tush and wriggle to the nearest full roll.

THE
EMPTY
ROLL
DUMP

You're going to be in there for a long time, so rather than count swan beaks on the wallpaper, you bring some reading material; as much as you feel is necessary, depending on the difficulty of the dump. If you leave the reading material, say, on a little table, it soon grows into a respectable library.

THE
LIBRARY
DUMP

You send the dump on its way.
It drops like a depth charge into
the bowl, creating a column of
cold bowl water that washes
your bottom with a startlingly
unpleasant shock. Now you're
wet and embarrassed. Blot
instead of wiping.

THE
SPLASH
BACK
DUMP

Pain, that's what this dump and childbirth have in common. It's simply a case of too much dump trying to go through too small a hole, and there's no obstetrician to help.

THE
CAESAREAN
DUMP

Thankfully, this dump doesn't happen very often, but once in a while we all have to grapple with a dump so tough, so stubborn that you get really red in the face applying enough pressure to force it out. It feels like either your top or your bottom will explode. Usually, your sphincter gives first, Thank God.

THE
MY HEAD
MIGHT
EXPLODE
DUMP

You're in-flight and the coffee
and croissants have caught
up with you. You join the 14
other airline breakfast victims
standing in line for an In-Flight
Dump. Aside from the obvious
discomforts associated with
the lavoratory on an airplane,
the most striking feature of the
whole event is there is no
water in the hopper until you
flush. So your dump just lies
there in an awful looking pile,
like what a dog did on the
sidewalk. And they don't give
you a pooper scooper, either.

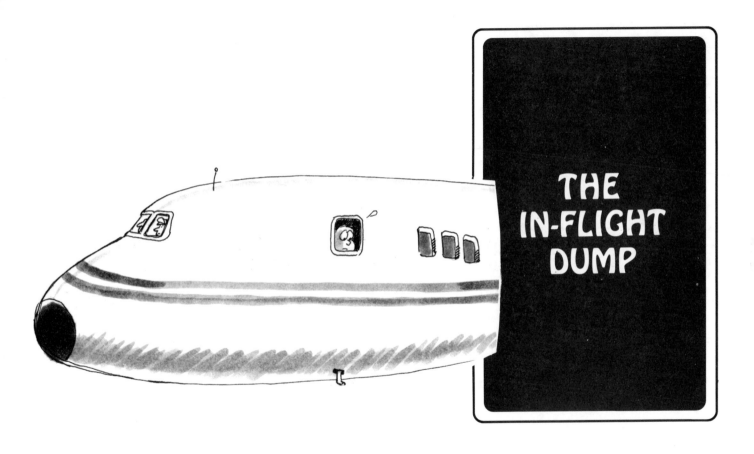

Everyone has had to go outdoors from time to time. This can be a rather pleasant experience, really. The open air, nature, and a good bush all contribute to the peaceful ambience that our primitive forefathers must have enjoyed. What can screw up this harmonious interlude is a troop of Brownies or a patch of poison ivy.

THE
ALFRESCO
DUMP

This is a dump that is simply too big to go through the aperture provided by nature for the purpose. You sit there, thinking over your dilemma. First, it hurts, and it isn't going to get better. You wonder if you'll ever see your loved ones again. You imagine newspaper headlines screaming "<u>Man Dies Trying to Hatch Monster Loaf!</u>" You realize you'll have to resolve the crisis before you leave the bathroom. Basically there are only three things you can do: 1. Scream 2. Call an Obstetricion or 3. Hope like hell you have enough vaseline to get you through it.

THE
CHILDBIRTH
DUMP

The toddler does a neat dump in his training pants. The toddler thinks it's wonderful. It's soft and sticky, but the real joy is that it's homemade. So, the toddler reaches into his pants takes the dump out and plays with it for a while. Then one of his parents says from the other room..."It's too quiet in there. What're you up to?" The toddler gets guilty and hides the dump. You find it 15 years later in an old pair of galoshes at the back of a closet you're cleaning out.

THE
TINY-TOT
DUMP

Hot when it goes in, and rocket fuel when it leaves. The Chili Dump stays with you all day, making your tush feel like a heat shield.

THE
CHILI
DUMP

In case you didn't know, a
latrine is a hole in the ground
with a tent around it where
soldiers, boy scouts and flies
go to dump. Tip: Don't ever,
ever, look in the hole.

THE
LATRINE
DUMP

You are in mid-dump and the phone rings. What do you do? Abort, that's what. Pinch it off, go for the phone, and save the rest for later. It isn't pretty but you've gotta do what you gotta do.

THE
ABORTED
DUMP

Every stall is filled. You're in the middle one trying to do your business quietly and get a move on out of there because there are people outside waiting to use your stall. Everything is relatively quiet, I mean aside from the fidgeting noises and toilet rolls being used and wiping noises. Suddenly, your dump explodes with a sharp report that sounds like the big cannon in the "Guns of Navarone". It's embarrassing, but it's just a Howitzer Dump. You wish there were an escape route down the pipes and into the sewer, but there isn't. You'll have to go out there and face them.

THE
HOWITZER
DUMP

The phrase "Shit Happens" really applies here in a big way. When the ice in your tainted margarita makes contact with your lower intestinal tract, the fun begins. For the next 72 hours you'd probably be better off if you carried your own portable toilet with you because you will spend most of that time on the pot and the rest of the time in a fetal position. Now you realize why Mexico never had a navy.

You do an industrial strength dump which requires some major wiping and then flush the entire pile. Suddenly, the whole mess begins to boil up the bowl toward you. If there is no plunger in the bathroom, it's best to run like hell.

You're just sitting there in a state of sublime peace when all of a sudden you emit a group of noisy gassy bursts that break the silence like machine gun fire. The guy in the next stall hits the floor like a combat veteran cradling his umbrella like an M-16. Damn commies.

You feel a noisy one coming on. Relatives, friends or work-mates are within earshot, so you must employ some clever techniques to cover the disgusting sounds you are about to emit. Timing is obviously very important here. At the precise moment of release, try the following sound effects:
1. Flush the toilet
2. Sing the first two stanzas of "The Battle Hymn of the Republic" or
3. Drop a handful of quarters on the floor.

THE
SOUND
EFFECT
DUMP

You go, and you've really gassed out the place. So, you reach for the English Lilac 'n Pine Forest Air Freshener spray can and spray the whole joint. Now the place smells like The Redwood Forest. Who do you think you're kidding?

You're running along, and the rhythmical bouncing motion of your stride acts on your intestines, activating them into a serious dump mode. So now your run takes on a significantly different meaning. You are now pitted against time and nature. If you run faster, your spasms will get worse, and if you slow down, you'll never make it home in time. Give up running or give up dumping.

You have enough on your mind when you're in the bathroom without worrying about a lockless door and someone bursting in to find you in mid-dump mode. So, how can you prevent this embarrassing spectacle from taking place? One way is to strategically place your foot against the door. If you can't do this, hum loudly.

THE
SECURITY
DUMP

You're in a cab or in an elevator, minding your own business, when you feel a little ripple of gas flutter its way innocently down to your tush. You hold it gently, not wanting to release it until you reach open air, but it sneaks out quietly. You realize immediately that something is drastically wrong because you feel warmth and moisture below. You have experienced a Surprise Dump. Now, you've got to get to a bathroom fast and spend the rest of the day without your underwear. Have a nice day.

THE
SURPRISE
DUMP

Corn for dinner tonight? Niblet
Dump tomorrow. I remember
my first Niblet Dump. I thought
my stomach must have gone on
vacation or something. Two cute
little loaves all polka dotted
with undigested corn niblets.
The green giant's revenge,
I guess.

THE
NIBLET
DUMP

Some unfortunate person goes into the bathroom after you've just left and says, "My God, what did you do in here?" What you did was an Environmental Protection Agency Dump. It's so bad looking you think it'll surely rot the pipes. It smells so foul that it could drop a moth in mid-flight. The bathroom should be sealed for at least 48 hours. The government may have some guidelines regarding this dump.

How does one describe a Turnpike Dump? As simply as possible, it's going to the bathroom where 50,000 motorists have dumped before you... this morning. With all that dumping there's bound to be problems, and believe me, there are. Unless it's an emergency, I'd just get a map and some gas and be on my way.

Baby makes a regular dump and goes on about his baby business, crawling, sitting, rolling and such. The dump acts like a piece of damp clay, changing shape everytime baby does something with his tush. When baby's diaper is eventually changed, what falls out of the diaper is a thing that looks like one of my Aunt Sophie's bran muffins.

THE
DIAPER
MUFFIN
DUMP

For the most part you've completed your dump, but there's one little morsel that refuses to drop off. You're getting impatient. Someone else wants to use your stall. So, you grip the seat with both hands and wriggle, twist, pump; but that last little stubborn piece just hangs there, suspended, clinging like a canned peach between you and the bowl water. Maybe the person pounding impatiently on the door has scissors.

THE
CLING-ON
DUMP

You go, then you stand up to flush, and the darn thing has disappeared! Where'd it go? Did it creep down the pipe? Did you dream the whole thing? Is it lurking just out of sight? Should you wipe? Maybe you should, to make sure you went. Should you flush? You'd better, because if you don't you know it'll reappear and smile at the next person who comes in.

Stuck in traffic after having 3 cups of coffee and a raisin bran muffin.

You feel so bad that you don't know which end of you to put down first. You have roaring cramps, so you sit down. Then a wave of nausea rolls over you like a cold fog, so you stand up. Then the cramps squeeze your intestines like a vice, so you sit down again. Up, down, up, down. Do you wish your mommy were close by?

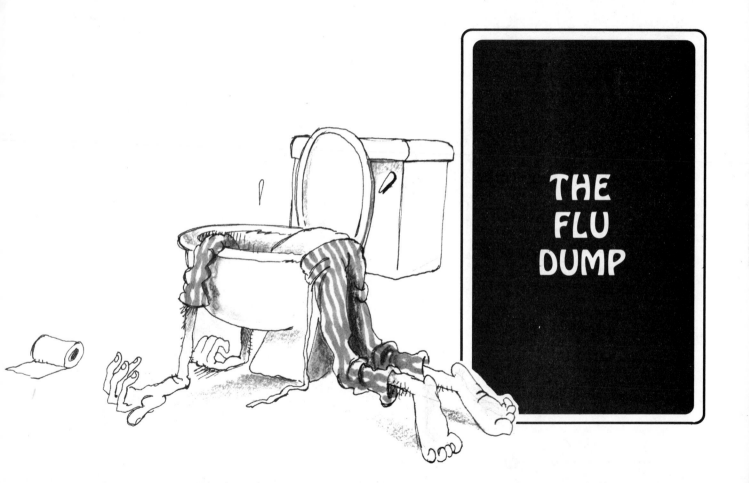

Construction workers and out-
door concert goers will tell you
about going in a portable toilet.
My best description would be,
it's like taking a shit in an upright
coffin. It's claustrophobic, and
it smells bad. Best advice, go in
a paper cup.

THE PORTA-POTTIE DUMP

Born from nacho cheese, gua-
camole and tortilla chips, the
After Burner Dump is a 5 alarm
nightmare. It sits there boiling
the inside of your intestines
until you release it frantically.
Then it leaves its rocket fuel
afterglow which will send you
to a cold shower for relief.

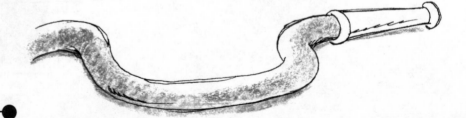

THE AFTER-BURNER DUMP

The scene is a public toilet...
You've got to go, but there's no
toilet seat, or the seat is so dirty
that the flies won't even land on
it. It's too late to go anyplace
else, so you must employ a
squat dump. You must bare
your derriere, take a pose re-
sembling a desperate football
lineman, and making sure your
tush is properly lined up with
the bowl - you aim and let go,
hoping your slacks don't get in
the way.

THE
SQUAT
DUMP

In the beginning, the Lord created the earth, the sky and the firmament; but I hope he didn't create this dump because there is nothing biblical about it.

In the beginning, it starts out as a normal movement, so you get on with it, and then you run out of gas. That's right, you run out of propulsion. The dump is right there at the end of your barrel and refuses to go any further. You grunt, you squeeze, you wriggle but it just stays there like a lump of lead. You've only got two choices here. One is to squeeze the damn thing back up your intestine and wait until next time. The other is to pretend you're a proctologist and go after it yourself. Not a pretty picture, is it?

THE
PROCT-
OLOGIST
DUMP

This one starts when a cigar chewing, wrench wielding, jumpsuited monkey with "Mitch" embroidered on his oily pocket hands you an oversized neon, plastic tagged restroom key, and it goes down hill from there. You have to carry that key, which acts like a poster advertising the fact that you have to go to all the other patrons waiting for gas. Then what you usually find is a suspiciously dank, poorly lit, foul smelling, tiled nightmare of a room. No toilet paper and cold running water - if you are lucky. You get on with what you're there for quickly, hoping no one busts in on you, and leave. No wonder no one wants to talk about it.

THE
GAS
STATION
DUMP

No matter how much you wipe, it doesn't seem to be enough. You blow the whole roll and you have to flush 25 times, too. The whole episode is an exercise in consumer waste.

You flush the dump, and the swirling motion of the receding bowl water forces the dump to the porcelain sides, scraping a creative squiggle on its way down. You flush again but the curlicue hangs in there. Love it or leave it, your choice.

Ahh, you're done. So you wipe, put yourself together, wash your hands and are about to vacate the bathroom when you feel another dump coming. You have to go for a curtain call. The world's record is 7.

THE
ENCORE
DUMP

This is a dump that's going so badly, you say "Lord, if I live through this, I'll take up religion!" You always get through it, but seldom keep the promise, because a Born Again Dump is like childbirth, you forget the pain quickly.

THE
BORN
AGAIN
DUMP

This is truly one of the sublime primal pleasures in our fast paced technological world. All you need is a good breakfast and a pot of coffee to get things started. It's Sunday; you can relax and retire to the bathroom, a big thick paper tucked under your arm. You spread out all the sections and plant yourself on the porcelain throne. Take some liesurely hours dumping and reading. You'll be a better person for it.

THE
SUNDAY
PAPER
DUMP

Any dump that requires the
use of professional services -
plumbing, pipe fitting,
welding, tiling or janitorial
assistance.

THE
PLUMBER'S
DUMP

Somebody forgets to put the seat down. It's late, you're sleepy or it's dark, and you plant your warm tush on the arctic cold bowl. You didn't think you could move that fast as you almost hit the ceiling.

THE
ICEBERG
DUMP

"Look mama, lady do Poo-Poo"...
The little toddler in the next stall
has poked his inquisitive head
under the partition and is point-
ing at you. You cringe, but don't
panic, and reach slowly into your
pocketbook and give the little
dear some lipstick to eat.

THE
PEEK-A-BOO
DUMP

Other books we publish are available at many fine stores. If you can't find them, send directly to us.

2400-How To Have Sex On Your Birthday. Finding a partner, special birthday sex positions, places to keep your birthday erection, faking the birthday orgasm, kinky sex on your birthday and much more.

2401-Is There Sex After Children? There are chapters on pre-teens and privacy, keeping toddlers out of your bedroom, great sex myths to tell your kids, how to have sex on a vacation, places to hide lingerie, where children come from, things kids bring to show and tell and more.

2402-Confessions From The Bathroom. There are things in this book that happen to all of us that none of us ever talk about. The Gas Station Dump, for example, or the Corn Niblet Dump, the Porta Pottie Dump, the Sunday Newspaper Dump to mention just a few.

2403-The Good Bonking Guide. Bonking is a great new British term for doing "you know what". Covers bonking in the dark, bonking with foreigners, bonking all night long, improving your bonking, kinky bonking and everything else you've ever wanted (or maybe didn't want) to know.

2404-Sex Slave: How To Find One, How To Be One. What it takes to be a Sex Slave, how to pick up Sex Slaves, the fine art of sexual groveling, 6 never-fail opening lines and 6 good things to know about break-away clothing -- and more than you ever imagined.

2405-Mid-Life Sex. Mid-Life Sex is taking all night to do what you used to do all night, talking your wife into visiting a nude beach, being tolerant of farts under the covers and having biological urges dwindle to an occasional nudge.

2406-World's Sex Records. Lists the greatest sex records of all time, including the world's most successful personal ad, the kinkiest bedroom, the most calories burned during sex, the cheapest escort service and the greatest sex in a car -- plus many more.

2407-40 Happens. When being out of prune juice ruins your whole day, you finally fulfill your book of the month commitment, you can no longer party for 24 hours straight and you realize anyone with the energy to do it on a weeknight must be a sex maniac.

2408-30 Happens. When you no longer party all night long, you take out a lifetime membership at your health club, and you still wonder when the baby fat will finally disappear.

2409-50 Happens. When you remember when "made in Japan" meant something that didn't work, and you can't remember what you went to the top of the stairs for.

2410-Bosom Buddies. Uncovered at last--the truth about women's bouncy parts: they're probably talking to each other! This book tells us what they would say, if only we could hear them!

2411-The Geriatric Sex Guide. It's not his mind that needs expanding, and you're in the mood now, but by the time you're naked, you won't be!

2412-Golf Shots. Humorously tells you how to look for lost balls, what excuses to use to play through first, ways to distract your opponent, and when and where a true golfer is willing to play golf.

2413-101 Ways to Improve Your Husband Or Wife. Covers how to keep your wife from losing your socks, teach your husband to clean a toilet, drive your wife crazy, and lots more.

2414-60 Happens. When your kids start to look middle-aged, when software is some kind of comfortable underwear, and when your hearing is perfect if everyone would just stop mumbling.

2415-Birthdays Happen. When you realize your Mom may not be the greatest cook, when your biological urges dwindle to an occasional nudge, and you realize that your hairline is not receding but that your forehead is growing.

2416-The Absolutely Worst Fart Book. What is the Absolutely Worst Fart? Is it The First Date Fart, The Oh My God Don't Let Me Fart Now Fart, The Lovers' Fart, The Doctor's Exam Room Fart? There are many many choices. You choose.

2417-Women Over 30 Are Better Because... Their nightmares about exams are starting to fade, their handbags can sustain life for about a week with no outside support whatsoever, and they can eat a double hot fudge sundae and not "break out".

2418-9 Months In The Sac. A humorous look at pregnancy through the eyes of the baby, such as: why do pregnant women have to go to the bathroom as soon as they get to the store, and why does baby start doing aerobics when it's time to sleep?

2419-Cucumbers Are Better Than Men Because... Cucumbers never miss the toilet, cucumbers are always ready when you are, cucumbers won't ask "how's your diet?" at the dinner table, and cucumbers will never hear "yes, yes" when you're saying "NO, NO."

2420-Happy Anniversary: A How To Book For Husbands And Wives. This book takes all those embarrassing moments, crazy quirks, and irritating habits of your spouse, and helps you laugh at them. Learn how to deal with passion on weeknights, bathroom habits, party antics, and much, much more.

2421-Honeymoon Guide. Every IMPORTANT thing to know about the honeymoon — from The Advantages Of Undressing With The Light On (it's slightly easier to undo a bra) to What Men Want Most (being allowed to sleep right afterwards without having to talk about love).

2422-Eat Yourself Healthy. Calories really add up if the food is consumed at a table. Snacking and stand up nibbling don't count. The four food groups are pizza, ice cream, chocolate, and egg rolls. Green M&M's are full of the same vitamins found in broccoli and lots of other useful eating information your mother never told you.

Ivory Tower Publishing Co., Inc.   125 Walnut St., Watertown, MA 02172   (617) 923-1111   **$7.00 postpaid**